THE SOLOMON R GUGGENHEIM MUSEUM

DISCOVERING ARCHITECTURE

EDUARD ALTARRIBA & BERTA BARDÍ I MILÀ

Button BOOKS

CONTENTS

KEY TO SYMBOLS

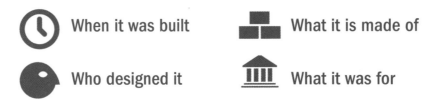

When it was built   What it is made of

Who designed it   What it was for

ACKNOWLEDGEMENTS **Eduard** Many thanks to everyone who has helped make this book a reality. To Meli, for her constant help in making this and all my other life projects bear fruit, and to Ariadna, Pere, and Lourdes for always being there. Thanks also to Jordi Prat of the UPC's publications service and to all at GMC. **Berta** I dedicate this book to my family and friends: to my parents and my three siblings; to Ginesta and Maiol for allowing me to fulfil my dream of becoming a mother; to Joan and Maria for sharing so many moments. To Eduard for his faith and generosity. To all the teachers I have had and who have transmitted to me the desire to learn and to improve myself. To Félix for believing in me more than I believed in myself. And, above all, to Daniel for his passion, his appreciation, and his boundless energy.

First published 2019 by Button Books, an imprint of Guild of Master Craftsman Publications Ltd, Castle Place, 166 High Street, Lewes, East Sussex, BN7 1XU, UK. Reprinted 2019. Text and illustrations © Berta Bardí i Milà and Eduard Altarriba, 2019. Copyright in the Work © GMC Publications Ltd, 2019. ISBN 978 1 78708 029 4. Distributed by Publishers Group West in the United States. All rights reserved. The right of Berta Bardí i Milà and Eduard Altarriba to be identified as the authors of this work has been asserted in accordance with the Copyright, Designs, and Patents Act 1988, sections 77 and 78. No part of this publication may be reproduced, stored in a retrieval system, or transmitted in any form or by any means without the prior permission of the publisher and copyright owner. While every effort has been made to obtain permission from the copyright holders for all material used in this book, the publishers will be pleased to hear from anyone who has not been appropriately acknowledged and to make the correction in future reprints. The publishers and authors can accept no legal responsibility for any consequences arising from the application of information, advice, or instructions given in this publication. A catalog record for this book is available from the British Library. Publisher: Jonathan Bailey. Production: Jim Bulley and Jo Pallett. Senior Project Editor: Wendy McAngus. Technical Consultant: Andrew Pearson. Translator: James Lupton. Managing Art Editor: Gilda Pacitti. Color origination by GMC Reprographics. Printed and bound in China.

Introduction

Throughout history humans have created shelters and places to protect themselves from bad weather and to keep safe from predators. Our early ancestors made their shelters with anything they had to hand, such as branches, leaves, or animal skins. Others dug holes in the ground for shelter or moved into caves. Over time, simple shelters evolved into homes, which became an important part of the culture of different groups of people scattered across the world.

These primitive forms of buildings soon became settlements and villages. The design—or architecture—of settlements was something that went beyond being just a home for a family and started to serve the group as a whole. This included the construction of buildings that served the whole community, such as temples and bath houses. People began to think about how to organize public spaces, such as the streets and squares or markets. From that time on, most of human existence, whether in small or large groups, has taken place surrounded by architecture.

This book is a journey through the ways that civilizations have approached building throughout history. The way we look at architecture today is the result of the work of architects who have built houses, temples, castles, skyscrapers, and palaces in the past. Nowadays, architects can learn from the past while creating new ideas and ways of thinking that help us to understand the world and transform it into a better, more habitable place.

The Pyramids

🕐 Around 2630 BC   ◐ Unknown   🧱 Mud bricks and stone   🏛 Tombs for pharaohs

The **Egyptian** pyramids are some of the most impressive monuments in the world. They were built as tombs for **pharaohs** who had died. Thousands upon thousands of workers were involved in the construction of the pyramids. The methods used in their construction were simple, precise, mathematical—and **mysterious**.

Ancient Egyptians believed that when pharaohs died they were transformed into immortal gods. The pyramids were built to guard their bodies, and each one was the resting place of their respected dead king. **Mummification** was performed to preserve the body, which was placed in a chamber that was then sealed forever.

The pyramids were made up of four equal isosceles triangles. These align with the four points of the compass, which meet at the summit.

Life after death

The Ancient Egyptians believed in life after death, and this affected both the way they lived and the way they died. Architects designed the spaces where the gods were honored after death, which would be their homes for eternity. The Egyptians dedicated a lot of effort and the best materials to the buildings associated with their gods, their rituals, and the afterlife.

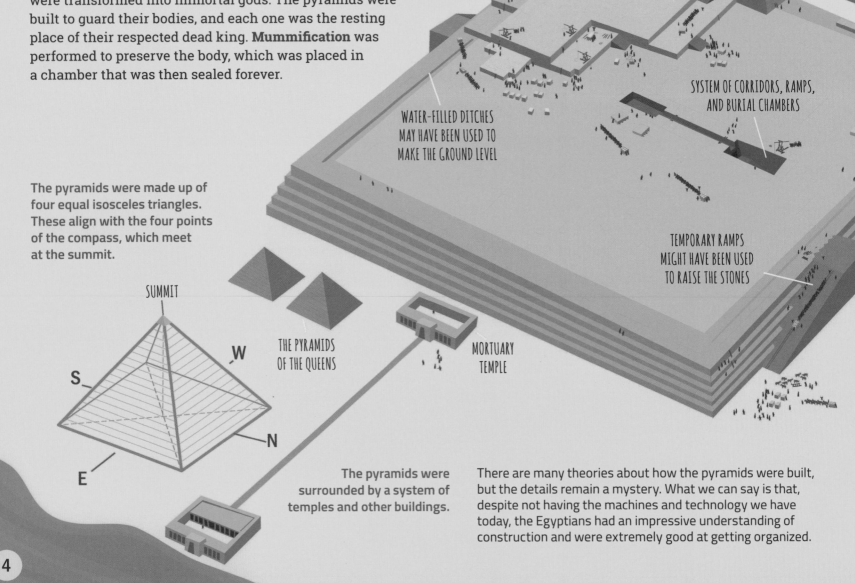

CONSTRUCTION OF THE EXTERNAL WALL

SYSTEM OF CORRIDORS, RAMPS, AND BURIAL CHAMBERS

WATER-FILLED DITCHES MAY HAVE BEEN USED TO MAKE THE GROUND LEVEL

TEMPORARY RAMPS MIGHT HAVE BEEN USED TO RAISE THE STONES

SUMMIT

W

S

N

E

THE PYRAMIDS OF THE QUEENS

MORTUARY TEMPLE

The pyramids were surrounded by a system of temples and other buildings.

There are many theories about how the pyramids were built, but the details remain a mystery. What we can say is that, despite not having the machines and technology we have today, the Egyptians had an impressive understanding of construction and were extremely good at getting organized.

EMBALMING CEREMONY

Some blocks were carved close to the site, while others were transported from far away along the River Nile.

WORKERS' VILLAGE

Builders might have used sleds to transport the stones from quarries. They would have watered the sand so the sleds could move better.

GODS, TOMBS, AND TEMPLES

Early civilizations used local materials such as wood, stone, or mud to build their structures. The Mesopotamians, for example, who lived between the rivers Tigris and Euphrates about 5,000 years ago, used mud to make bricks to build their towns and cities.

Religion was very important in early societies. This led to them making their religious buildings bigger and bigger and using longer-lasting materials such as stone.

In an effort to get closer to the gods, some buildings—such as ziggurats and pyramids—were built to reach into the sky. Some of these buildings, which can still be seen today, show the power of the kings and pharaohs who ordered them to be built.

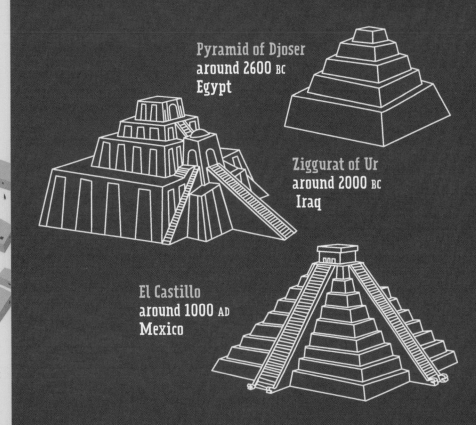

Pyramid of Djoser
around 2600 BC
Egypt

Ziggurat of Ur
around 2000 BC
Iraq

El Castillo
around 1000 AD
Mexico

⚙ ARCHITRAVE ARCHITECTURE

This is the simplest way to build structures. **Vertical columns** are joined to **horizontal beams**, called architraves. No mortar is used, and it is largely the force of **gravity** that keeps the architrave in place.

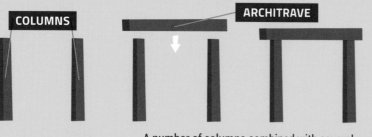

COLUMNS

ARCHITRAVE

A number of columns combined with several architraves make up a structure.

Architraves are also used to bear weight in walls, which allows doors and windows to be built.

The greatest force is applied in the center of an architrave. This means that if columns are too far apart or too much weight is placed on the structure, it may become distorted or break.

First you need to calculate how much force the materials can bear.

Imitating wood

At first, the Ancient Greeks used wood to build their temples. When they started to use stone architraves, they copied the shapes they had used in their earlier temples.

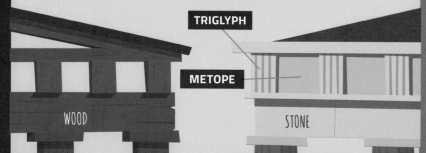

TRIGLYPH

METOPE

WOOD

STONE

The Parthenon Athens, Greece

🕐 447–432 BC   ◔ Phidias, Ictino, and Callicrates   ▦ Marble   🏛 Shrine

The Parthenon is in a style known as **Doric** and is located at the highest point of the **Acropolis**, the "high city" of Athens. It was dedicated to Athena, the goddess of wisdom and war.

When it was built, Athens was the center of Ancient Greek art and culture. The Acropolis started out as a fortress, but in time it was converted into a **sacred place**. While the Parthenon was the most important temple, there were other sacred places there, too.

ARCHITRAVE

TRIGLYPH

COLUMN

THE WIDE COLUMNS PROVIDE THE BASIC STRUCTURE.

PLATFORM

PHIDIAS was one of the Parthenon architects. He was also a sculptor famous for carving a huge statue of the goddess Athena in ivory and gold.

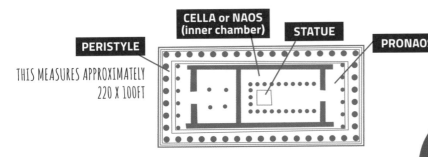

PERISTYLE

THIS MEASURES APPROXIMATELY 220 X 100FT

CELLA or NAOS (inner chamber)

STATUE

PRONAOS

Beautiful, important, and expensive

Religion dominated the lives of the Greeks. People went to temples and sanctuaries to ask the gods for favors. They offered gold, silver, and sacrificial animals to the gods. They organized festivals and sporting events in their honor. In return, they expected their gods to protect them from disease and look after their crops.

Only priests were allowed to enter the temple.

CAPITAL

DORIC   **IONIC**   **CORINTHIAN**

The Greeks used **proportion** to try to achieve visual perfection. This led to the beginning of architectural **orders**, which described a style of building and the relationship between its different parts. The **capital** (top of a column) is the part of the building that best shows which order it is.

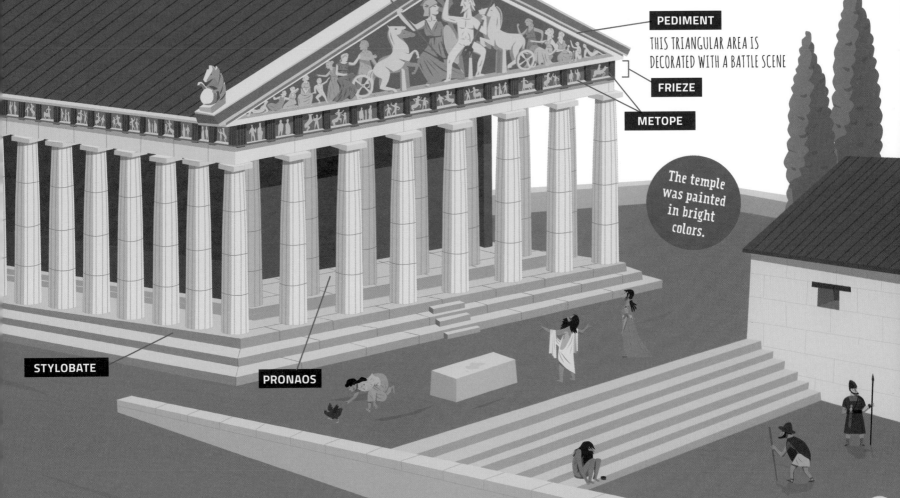

PEDIMENT

THIS TRIANGULAR AREA IS DECORATED WITH A BATTLE SCENE

FRIEZE

METOPE

The temple was painted in bright colors.

STYLOBATE

PRONAOS

THERMAL BATHS

As few Roman homes had bathrooms, thermal baths were places where people met socially and kept themselves clean. Romans could also exercise, play, talk with friends, relax, or read in the library. The baths played an important part in the lives of Romans, who spent many hours there every day.

The CARDO and DECUMANUS were the main streets in the city. They were built running north to south and east to west. Town gates were built where these streets passed through the walls.

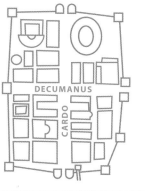

DECUMANUS

CARDO

FORUM

All Roman cities had a forum—a public space that served as a market square and meeting place. Positioned where the *cardo* and *decumanus* crossed, it was lined with the important religious and civic buildings so political gatherings and debates happened here.

MARKET

PUBLIC WATER FOUNTAIN

Roads were paved thoroughfares that linked all the cities in the Empire with Rome in Italy.

ROMAN ROAD

AQUEDUCT

An aqueduct is a structure used by the Romans to supply their cities with water, which frequently came from a long way away.

BASILICA

This was a building where legal and business activities were carried out, as well as official ceremonies, so it was not unlike a modern-day town hall. Basilicas were often built using columns that divided the space inside, creating long passageways between arcades. The central passage was usually wider and taller than those on either side.

The Romans buried their dead outside the city walls, usually beside the roads.

GYMNASIUM

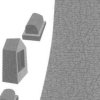

The birth of town planning

The Romans founded many cities throughout their empire. At each foundation ceremony the city limits were mapped out, showing where the walls would be built. The *cardo* and the *decumanus*—the main streets that crossed to divide the city into four—were shown. Residential blocks (*insulae*) and public buildings were built in each section. Basic services such as drinking water and sewers were also planned.

THEATER This was a semicircular building housing a stage with seating for the audience.

The **AMPHITHEATER** was a building used to stage public events, like a modern stadium. It hosted battles between gladiators and wild beasts, and it might be flooded with water so that naval battles could be re-enacted.

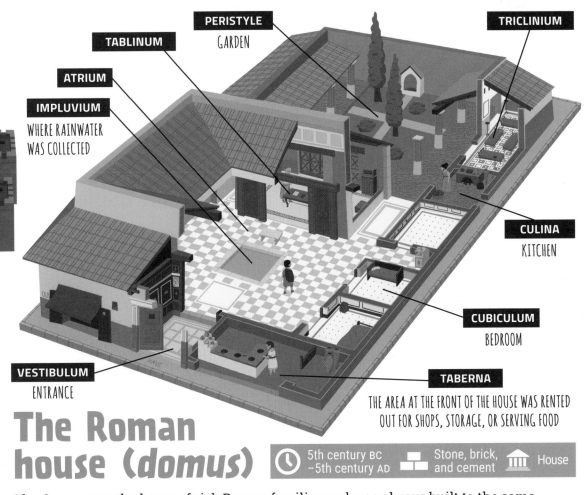

PERISTYLE GARDEN

TABLINUM

TRICLINIUM

ATRIUM

IMPLUVIUM WHERE RAINWATER WAS COLLECTED

CULINA KITCHEN

CUBICULUM BEDROOM

VESTIBULUM ENTRANCE

TABERNA THE AREA AT THE FRONT OF THE HOUSE WAS RENTED OUT FOR SHOPS, STORAGE, OR SERVING FOOD

The Roman house (domus)

🕐 5th century BC –5th century AD | 🧱 Stone, brick, and cement | 🏛 House

The domus was the home of rich Roman families and was always built to the same layout. There were no windows on to the outside world, but the rooms and living areas opened on to internal patios and gardens, which provided light and air. The atrium, an open-roofed entrance hall, was at the front of the house, with bedrooms leading off it. Behind was the tablinum, where the head of the household would receive guests. This was connected to the second part of the house—the rear garden, known as the peristyle. The dining area, or triclinium, was furnished with couches to lie on while eating.

⚙ ARCHES AND VAULTS

Arches are used to make doorways and windows and to open up spaces between supporting columns.

Arches are built using a number of pieces known as **voussoirs**, which support each other to make the arch. The voussoirs may be made of stone, brick, or any other material, although nowadays arches are also made of a single piece of concrete. The central voussoir, which completes the curve and keeps all the others from falling down, is known as the **keystone**.

Erecting a building is a struggle against gravity. The weight of the walls applies force to the arch, whose shape transmits this pressure toward the sides.

If the arch is not firmly supported on both sides, it can split and fall down. Because of this, **buttresses** are used in some buildings to redirect this sideways pressure into the ground.

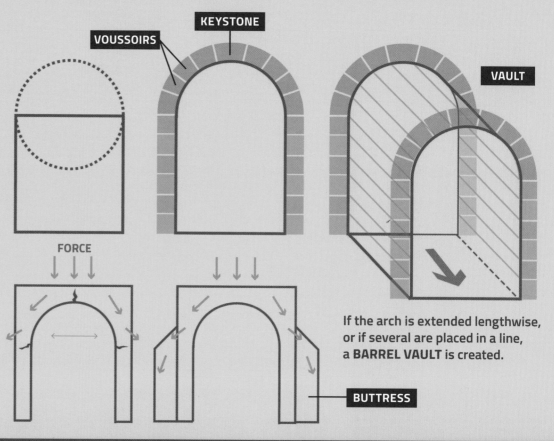

VOUSSOIRS

KEYSTONE

VAULT

FORCE

BUTTRESS

If the arch is extended lengthwise, or if several are placed in a line, a **BARREL VAULT** is created.

Kinds of arch

SEMICIRCULAR HORSESHOE GOTHIC OGEE POINTED TREFOIL

⚙ DOMES

Rotating an arch around its central point produces a dome, which is a bit like the way a barrel vault is formed.

Domes have been used since Roman times in large buildings such as temples, palaces, and thermal baths. The dome of the Pantheon in Rome is one of the best examples of a building constructed using traditional techniques.

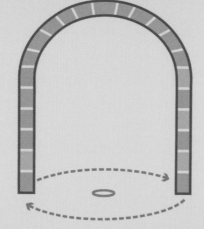
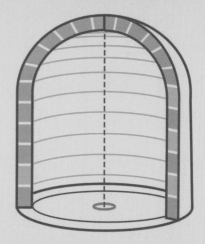

The Pantheon  Rome, Italy

🕐 118–125 AD | ◐ Apollodorus of Damascus | ▭ Concrete and brick | 🏛 Temple

The word Pantheon means "temple of all the gods." The building had a religious purpose but was also used for political meetings. It consists of a large circular space (the **rotunda**) topped by a dome. The only opening is at the top (the **oculus**). The oculus provides light and also functions as a ring that holds the structure together.

Geometry

The elementary geometric forms of the sphere and the cylinder were used to construct the dome and the rotunda. The height of the cylinder is equal to the radius of the sphere.

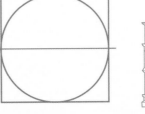

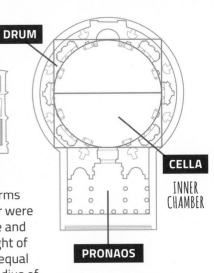

DRUM

CELLA

INNER CHAMBER

PRONAOS

OCULUS

DOME

The dome is made up of an inner and an outer concrete layer. It has a diameter of 142ft, making it the largest unreinforced concrete dome ever built.

COFFERED CEILING

The decorative indented panels also reduce the weight of the roof.

ROTUNDA

The rotunda is a cylinder made of two layers of brick reinforced with stone.

The Pantheon was later converted into a church and is still standing. If you go to Rome you can visit it!

The Pantheon was so well built that it has lasted for 19 centuries with almost no repairs.

M·AGRIPPA·L·FCO

The principal chamber is entered through the pronaos, which is shaped like a temple. This entrance space acts as a transition between the outside and the inside.

PRONAOS

Building with concrete

The Romans used concrete to construct their buildings. This was a mixture of water, volcanic rock, powdered brick, and limestone.

Byzantine architecture

The power of the Roman Empire was inherited by the city of Constantinople—later known as Byzantium, and today called Istanbul. The Byzantine Empire combined the culture of Rome with that of the Middle East. Some of the typical features of Byzantine architecture include the use of domes, bricks instead of stone, and a building system that was strong enough to place a dome on top of a building.

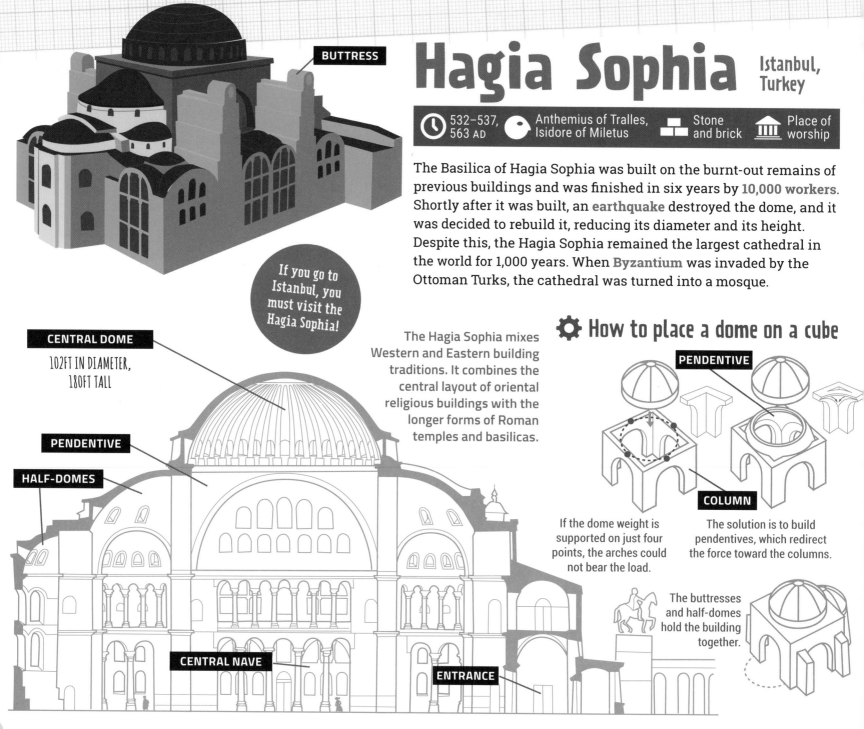

BUTTRESS

Hagia Sophia
Istanbul, Turkey

| 🕐 532–537, 563 AD | 👁 Anthemius of Tralles, Isidore of Miletus | 🧱 Stone and brick | 🏛 Place of worship |

The Basilica of Hagia Sophia was built on the burnt-out remains of previous buildings and was finished in six years by **10,000 workers**. Shortly after it was built, an **earthquake** destroyed the dome, and it was decided to rebuild it, reducing its diameter and its height. Despite this, the Hagia Sophia remained the largest cathedral in the world for 1,000 years. When **Byzantium** was invaded by the Ottoman Turks, the cathedral was turned into a mosque.

If you go to Istanbul, you must visit the Hagia Sophia!

CENTRAL DOME

102FT IN DIAMETER, 180FT TALL

PENDENTIVE

HALF-DOMES

CENTRAL NAVE

ENTRANCE

The Hagia Sophia mixes Western and Eastern building traditions. It combines the central layout of oriental religious buildings with the longer forms of Roman temples and basilicas.

⚙ How to place a dome on a cube

PENDENTIVE

COLUMN

If the dome weight is supported on just four points, the arches could not bear the load.

The solution is to build pendentives, which redirect the force toward the columns.

The buttresses and half-domes hold the building together.

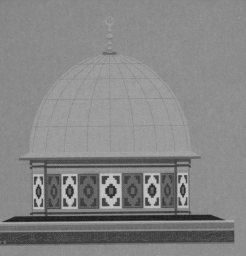

Dome of the Rock in
Jerusalem, Israel, Palestine

Blue Mosque
in Istanbul, Turkey

St Mark's Basilica
in Venice, Italy

Imam Khomeini Mosque
in Isfahan, Iran

A WORLD OF DOMES

Hagia Sophia was inspired by the dome of the Pantheon and was itself a model for all the domes that were built later. All along the Silk Road, in the Islamic world or in Christian Europe, the most important religious and political buildings have been crowned with domes.

St Basil's Cathedral
in Moscow, Russia

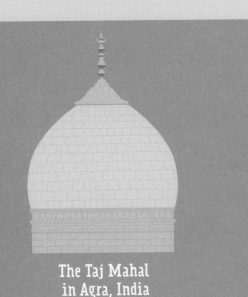

The Taj Mahal
in Agra, India

Tilya-Kori Madrasah
in Samarkand, Uzbekistan

St Paul's Cathedral
in London, United Kingdom

13

Andrea PALLADIO

Palladio (1508–1580) was an important Italian architect of the 16th century, toward the end of the **Renaissance**, a time of great art. He worked around the cities of **Venice** and **Vicenza**. His buildings, especially his **villas**, had a huge influence on the way later architects designed public buildings. They were inspired by Palladio's balanced classical style, which was based on **geometry, symmetry, and repetition**.

European thinkers and artists of the 16th century believed that the rediscovery of Graeco-Roman art and thought had led to a rebirth, or "renaissance," of classical culture.

La Rotonda Vicenza, Italy

🕐 1566–1620	⬤ Andrea Palladio	🧱 Stone	🏛 Country house

Villa Almerico Capra, better known as La Rotonda, is one of Palladio's most famous buildings. Located near Vicenza, it was built in the **Renaissance style**, using elements drawn from classical Greek and Roman temples. Though the name of the building means "round villa," in fact the foundation is a perfect square placed on top of a regular Greek cross.

Some of the most important concepts used by architects in their buildings are found in La Rotonda.

Rhythm

Rhythm refers to the order and size of objects in a building in relation to each other. As in music, the features are arranged according to a particular rhythm. For example, all the windows may be the same size and equally spaced, or they might be arranged differently or in no clear order at all.

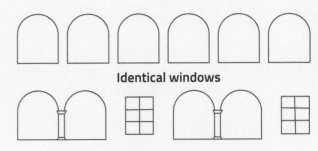

Identical windows

Varied windows gives a different rhythm

Symmetry

When one half of an object is a mirror image of the other half, that is symmetry. The concept of symmetry is found in both mathematics and nature. Our own bodies have symmetry too, and since ancient times it has been believed that buildings that are symmetrical transmit balance and beauty.

Today it is accepted that a house can be symmetrical, asymmetrical, or a mix of the two concepts.

Geometry

Geometry is a branch of mathematics that considers solid shapes. Buildings are solid forms—such as cubes, spheres (see the Pantheon, page 11), pyramids, or rectangular prisms. The final form of all buildings is the result of bringing together all these shapes.

Beauty

Palladio searched for beauty among the Renaissance ideals of geometry and proportion. Although these ideals have differed over time and across different cultures, *Vitruvius*, a Roman architect and theorist, argued that fine architecture rests on a balance between three principles: *venustas* (beauty), *firmitas* (strength), and *utilitas* (functionality).

The Japanese house

According to the Japanese, a beautiful house should be **empty**. Its floor, roof, walls, and structure should be visible, and it should have **no additional decoration**. For this reason, traditional Japanese houses are made up of a collection of rooms with no specific furniture. **Any activity**, such as eating, sleeping, or reading, may be carried out in **any room**. Only some spaces, such as the kitchen and the bathroom, have specific uses. All the other rooms are neutral and closely interconnected with each other and outside by sliding doors.

Houses are mainly built using wood from the forests of inland Japan. Wood is a long-lasting material that produces a sense of warmth.

Bamboo, paper, and cardboard are the principal materials used to build the thin walls of the house and the sliding doors.

The house is constructed using a wooden frame. Its columns and beams are the only form of decoration.

VERANDA

Since the 19th century Japanese style has influenced the art and architecture of the West. Modern architecture owes much to the simple, undecorated aesthetics of the East where buildings are organized around modular spaces, which can be expanded and adapted. This approach has had an important influence on architects such as Charles Rennie Mackintosh.

It is traditional for people to remove their shoes before entering a house, and to place them in the entrance (or *genkan*).

The importance of the garden

The garden is one of the most important aspects of traditional Japanese architecture. A good Japanese garden follows rules drawn from Zen Buddhist philosophy, which indicate where stones, water features, and plants should be placed. The idea is that the inside of the house should form a harmonious whole with nature. This is why verandas, porches, and sliding doors are so important—they provide a direct relationship between the rooms indoors and the outside world.

TEA HOUSE

Tea houses are small buildings used to perform the tea ceremony. They are usually decorated with seasonal flowers and are used for reflection and contemplation.

Instead of beds and sofas the Japanese use futons and cushions. These are stored in cupboards when not in use, leaving the room free for other purposes.

KITCHEN

Japanese houses are usually constructed on wooden platforms that raise them above the ground.

The measurements used in traditional Japanese houses are based on *tatami* floor mats, which are always twice as long as they are wide. Different combinations of tatami mats define the size of the different rooms in the house.

TATAMIS

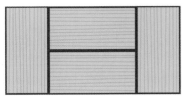
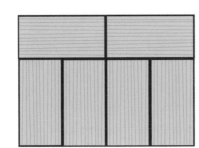

Katsura Imperial Villa
Kyoto, Japan

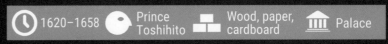

🕐 1620–1658	◉ Prince Toshihito	▦ Wood, paper, cardboard	🏛 Palace

This palace is one of the most important examples of Japanese art and architecture. The building work was started on the banks of the River Katsura near Tokyo by Prince Toshihito 400 years ago. The palace took 50 years to complete.

A KATSURA TEA HOUSE

The palace is a single-story building sitting on an enormous wooden platform. The main building (or *shoin*) is like a labyrinth made up of many rooms that are surrounded by pavilions and tea houses. The *shoin* was enlarged over time with the addition of more and more rooms, interconnected by sliding doors.

Japanese emperors and their families used the Katsura to withdraw from court life, rest, and look at the moon. The simple architecture and gardens that surround the palace aim to create a feeling of unity, harmony, and peace.

Most of the palace's rooms open outwards so that people can enjoy the gardens and the lake. The palace has a large number of outdoor passageways that wind through the gardens. There is even a platform in the garden that was designed to allow contemplation of the moon (*engawa*).

Architecture without architects

VERNACULAR ARCHITECTURE

When human beings first made homes for themselves they picked places that were close to rivers and on higher ground to be safe from potential enemies and dangerous animals. These settlements were not mapped out beforehand and had no architects or town planners to decide where streets and houses should be. Generation after generation of people shaped their communities by using their common sense, knowledge, and the materials they could find nearby. This is what we now know as vernacular architecture. Today, this type of architecture may still be found in rural areas and also in large cities.

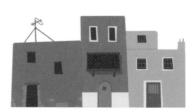

Although not created by a single person, vernacular buildings usually share the characteristics of other structures nearby. The houses found in a region tend to be similar to each other. They share the **same climate**, the **same culture**, and **similar materials**. Over time, the houses in a village are **extended** or **pulled down** so new ones can be built to replace them. But the same construction techniques, materials, textures, and colors are used with the result that, though each house is different, **a single architectural style** is maintained.

Architecture is rather like civilization in general: it is the sum of many individual parts that are shared and drawn together by culture.

⚙ How to build a rammed earth wall

In vernacular architecture drawings are not made before building starts —it just begins. Building techniques are a part of the culture of every place where people are found. One example is rammed earth walls.

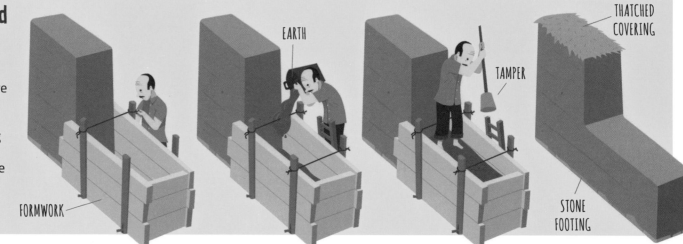

FORMWORK

EARTH

TAMPER

THATCHED COVERING

STONE FOOTING

This **Berber village** in Morocco's Atlas Mountains is an example of vernacular architecture. It is built using **stone walls** and **rammed earth** or mud on a mountainside in a hot, dry climate. It might look as if it has been thought out in advance, because all the houses are **similar in shape**, use the **same materials**, and frequently **share walls and roofs**. But this village has been built over many generations, creating the style that is characteristic of Berber vernacular architecture.

Yurt, Mongolia

Dacha, Russia

Dani tribal hut, Papua New Guinea

Tepee, American Great Plains

HOMES

From the caves lived in by the first humans to the modern houses of today, each culture has created different kinds of home to provide a safe place to shelter using the materials available. Given the variations in climate and landscape across the world, it's not surprising how different these dwellings have turned out to be.

Adobe house, Al Hamra, Oman

Favela (slum) house, Brazil

Masia, Southern France and Northern Spain

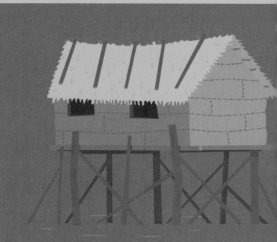

Sea gypsy stilt house, Sabah, Malaysia

Half-timbered house, UK

Inuit igloo, Canada

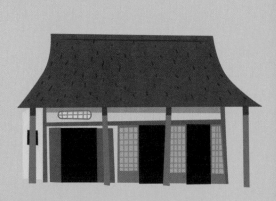

Tea house, Japan

Vardo Romany caravan, UK

Sampan, China

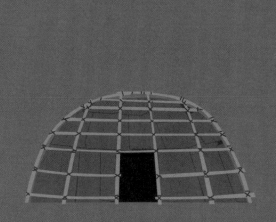

Wigwam, North America

Hut of the Podoko people, Cameroon

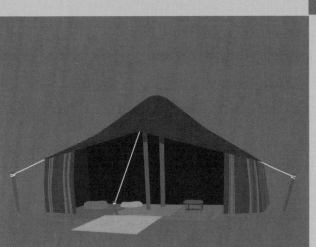

Nomadic dwelling, Moroccan desert

Log cabin, USA

A NEW AGE

The Industrial Revolution and the invention of the steam engine led to huge changes in architecture and engineering. The development of cast iron in factories meant new methods of construction came about. New ways of making materials, such as the ability to make large sheets of glass, replaced the old and transformed how buildings could be both imagined and built.

Iron began to be used to build factories, bridges, and other structures, but it also quickly became the material of choice for the most important buildings and monuments of the era.

For the first time it was possible to design and plan the mass production of the parts that make up a building before work began. The iron or glass sections were made in different factories and transported to the building site.

Using these new techniques architects and engineers were able to imagine vast, airy spaces bathed in light. Enormous exhibition pavilions were built during the 19th century, such as the famous Crystal Palace built for the Great Exhibition of 1851 in London. The Eiffel Tower was a huge metal structure designed by Stephen Sauvestre and built by the engineer Gustave Eiffel for the 1889 Exposition Universelle held in Paris.

Soon after the arrival of Robert Stephenson's *Rocket* (one of the first steam engines), the UK was covered by a network of railways.

The World's Fairs
These events were held in cities around the world and gave an opportunity to show off the technical and scientific advances of each country. The different nations competed to create the most spectacular buildings and monuments.

Four people were needed for the riveting process

The plan was to take the Eiffel Tower down after the exhibition finished, but it was decided to keep it. Now it is one of the most visited monuments in the world.

About 2.5 million rivets were used to join 18,000 pieces of iron to construct the Eiffel Tower.

⚙ Using rivets to join sheet metal

During the 19th century a large number of metal structures were made using metal sheets joined by rivets. Rivets are bolt-shaped pieces of metal, similar to nails. They were heated in coal-fired furnaces and when red hot they were inserted through pre-cut holes made in the metal sheets. The protruding ends were hammered until the two sheets were joined.

RED-HOT RIVET

HOLD WITH PINCERS

STRIKE WITH HAMMER

RED-HOT RIVET HEAD

Crystal Palace London, UK

🕐 1851 ◖ Joseph Paxton ▥ Cast iron and glass 🏛 Exhibition pavilion

The Crystal Palace in London was an example of "cast-iron architecture" and the classic symbol of the World's Fairs. The British illustrator and landscape architect Joseph Paxton designed a building that was ground-breaking for its time: an enormous greenhouse a third of a mile long, that was built using repeated metal structures and panes of glass that were organized in three long aisles about 110ft high.

ART NOUVEAU

Art Nouveau or "new art" was a late 19th century European style that valued craftsmanship and detail. The look varied from country to country but generally aimed to bring together art and crafts in architecture. Some of its pioneers were the architect Victor Horta and the painters Alphonse Mucha and Gustav Klimt. Art Nouveau architecture makes use of natural forms and curved lines. Its artistic style is also found in windows, sculpture, furniture, jewelry, lamps, prints, and graphic design. It is considered to be an all-embracing style that creates a welcoming environment.

Art Nouveau Metro entrance in Paris

METROPOLITAIN

Art Deco: Chrysler Building in New York by William Van Alen

Inspired by Art Nouveau and the artistic avant garde, the Art Deco style also placed great emphasis on the decorative arts and design using geometric forms and straight lines. It created a style associated with luxury and glamor.

Nature as inspiration

Gaudí used shapes and structures inspired by nature. The curves he drew were forms that could be found in the natural world. In his buildings we might find a ceiling covered in waves, a wall of fish scales, a pillar that looks like a bone, or a roof shaped like a dragon's back.

Columns like a forest

Gaudí wanted the columns inside his church to be like a forest of trees.

DID YOU KNOW?
Building started on the Sagrada Família over 100 years ago and it is still not finished!

Once the central tower has been completed, the Sagrada Família will be the tallest church in the world.

THE OCHRE PARTS HAVE ALREADY BEEN BUILT.

Sagrada Família Barcelona, Spain

🕐 Started in 1902	◉ Antoni Gaudí	🧱 Stone, concrete and glass	🏛 Place of worship

Although it is yet to be completed, the Basilica of the Sagrada Família is Gaudí's best-known work. This spectacular church brings together sculpture, painting, and architecture to create a magical building. Inspired by his religious beliefs, Gaudí intended the Sagrada Família to be the greatest religious building in the world. He wanted to explain the history of Christianity using symbols and codes hidden throughout the building.

Trencadís

Gaudí invented a wall covering he called *trencadís*, which involves making a mosaic with pieces of broken tile (trencadís means "chopped up" in Gaudí's native language of Catalan). The advantage of this technique is that it is perfect for making designs on the curved shapes Gaudí used in his buildings.

THE BLUE PARTS HAVE NOT BEEN COMPLETED YET.

Antoni
GAUDÍ

ANTONI GAUDÍ

The architecture by Antoni Gaudí (1852–1926) is some of the most original in history. Most of his work is found in the Catalonian region of Spain. In his projects he used a lot of curves and wave-like patterns inspired by nature and the laws of geometry. But he also designed the minutest details of his buildings: everything from the front railings to the furniture, fireplaces, banisters, and lamps.

GOTHIC ARCH

PARABOLIC ARCH

WEIGHTS

STRINGS

MIRROR

⚙ The upside-down building

Many of Gaudí's buildings use **parabolic arches**, which allow very tall structures to be built. In the 19th century, without the benefit of computers, it was very hard to calculate curves of this kind. Gaudí invented a system to work out the form his arches should take and the loads they would be able to bear. He made models using string to represent the arches and weights to simulate the load. But what is so brilliant is that he did this by hanging his model from the ceiling above a mirror, which he could look into to see what the building would look like once completed.

When architecture meets other arts

The role of the architect involves imagining and building our future environment. This includes its buildings, parks, housing estates, and cities. But many architects want to be responsible for **all aspects** of the design, from the **largest** and most complex elements to the **smallest**, simplest things within it.

When architects turn their hands to all aspects of a building, this may include everything from display cabinets and furniture to door handles and cutlery.

Dining room chair
from the Batlló House
by Antoni Gaudí,
1907

PH5 pendant lamp
by Poul Henningsen,
1958

Ladderback chair
from Hill House
by Charles Rennie
Mackintosh,
1903

Sitzmaschine chair
by Josef Hoffmann,
1905

Wiggle chair
by Frank Gehry,
1972

Teapot
by Walter Gropius,
1969

Architects Alvar
Aalto and Aino
Marsio-Aalto in
their home studio
(1934–36)

FROM LAMPS TO CITIES

Sometimes we might confuse architects with designers, engineers, landscape designers, or town planners. An architect works with all kinds of buildings and the objects they contain, but is also involved with public spaces and town planning.

Egg chair by Arne
Jacobsen, 1958

Øresund Bridge, between
Denmark and Sweden,
1999

A **designer** might focus on designing objects, products, concepts, or spaces. Some specialize in furniture and items for the home such as chairs, tables, lamps, cutlery, and glasses. Many architects are also interested in developing these aspects in their own buildings.

Structural and civil engineers are responsible for the more technical aspects of the design of a town or city, such as structural calculations for bridges, planning road routes, or designing ports.

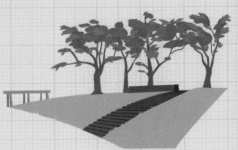

Residential square, Barcelona

The Woodland Cemetery,
Stockholm, Sweden by Erik
Gunnar Asplund, 1915

People who plan cities are called **town planners**. Their job covers the environment, transport, public spaces, and the buildings in the town. The town planner looks at the urban space and tries to make it a better place for people to live in.

Landscape designers study and plan large spaces, looking at them from an artistic and architectural viewpoint. They can change the landscape by using subtle or sometimes invasive techniques.

Le CORBUSIER

Le Corbusier (1887–1965) was born Charles-Édouard Jeanneret in Switzerland. He lived in Paris for many years and designed buildings around the world. He concentrated on architecture and town planning but was also a painter and sculptor. His goal was to create a modern form of architecture that was very different from traditional forms, and he is considered one of the most influential architects of the 20th century.

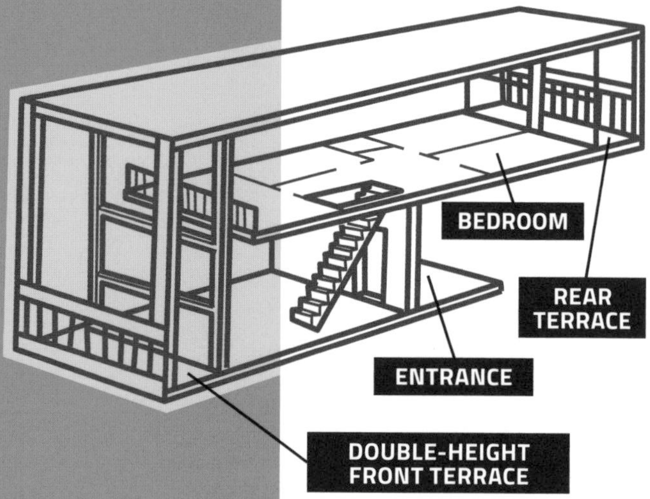

BEDROOM

REAR TERRACE

ENTRANCE

DOUBLE-HEIGHT FRONT TERRACE

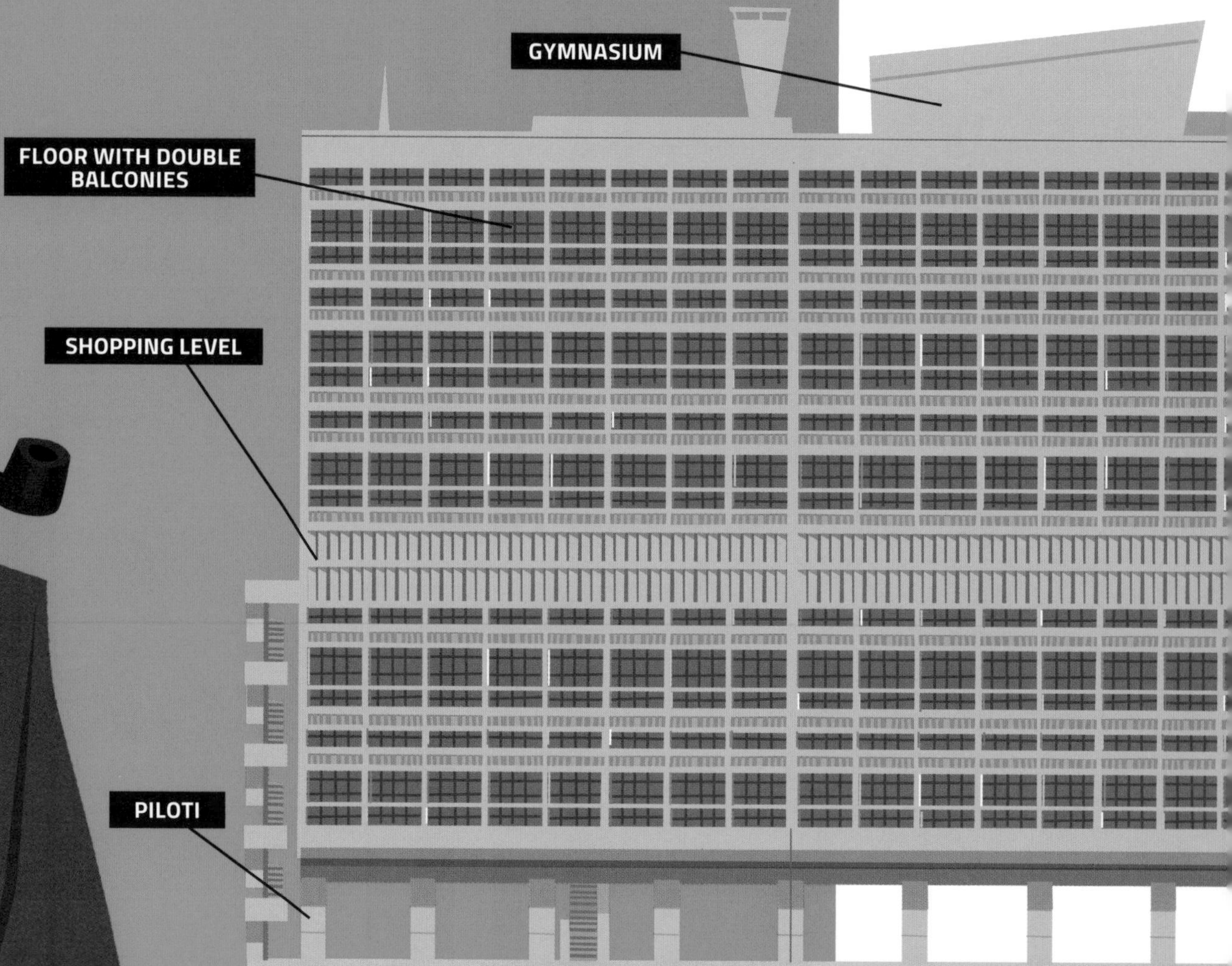

GYMNASIUM

FLOOR WITH DOUBLE BALCONIES

SHOPPING LEVEL

PILOTI

Unité d'habitation
Marseilles, France

1946–52   Le Corbusier

Concrete   Homes and communal areas

28

The Modulor

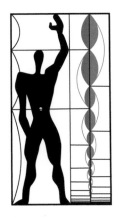

Le Corbusier created a system of **measurements** called the Modulor based on the **human body** and on **geometry**. His scale was based on a man standing with his arm raised and the belly button at the exact center. The figure is drawn within two overlapping rectangles 3ft 8in wide and 7ft 4in high. He combined these measurements with the **Golden Ratio** (a harmonious division of space dating back to Ancient Greek times), creating a measurement system that he used in his architectural activities.

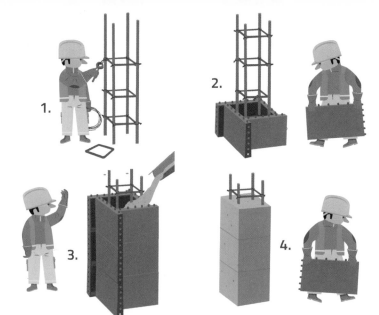

COMMUNAL TERRACE

CAFETERIA

⚙ Making a reinforced concrete column

1. Preparing the steel reinforcing bars 2. Making the formwork
3. Filling with concrete 4. Removing the formwork.

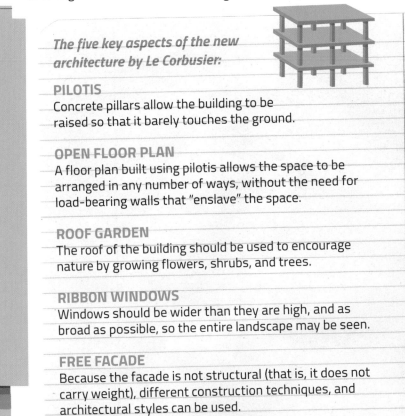

The five key aspects of the new architecture by Le Corbusier:

PILOTIS
Concrete pillars allow the building to be raised so that it barely touches the ground.

OPEN FLOOR PLAN
A floor plan built using pilotis allows the space to be arranged in any number of ways, without the need for load-bearing walls that "enslave" the space.

ROOF GARDEN
The roof of the building should be used to encourage nature by growing flowers, shrubs, and trees.

RIBBON WINDOWS
Windows should be wider than they are high, and as broad as possible, so the entire landscape may be seen.

FREE FACADE
Because the facade is not structural (that is, it does not carry weight), different construction techniques, and architectural styles can be used.

The Unité d'habitation is a series of buildings in different cities. The first was built in Marseilles where Le Corbusier created communal living for around 2,000 people. The inhabitants were provided with all the basic services they needed. They were surrounded by nature, and their living spaces were designed for families, with balconies and double-height living spaces.

Fallingwater
Mill Run, Pennsylvania, USA

🕐 1936–39 ● Frank Lloyd Wright 🧱 Stone, concrete, and glass 🏛 House

The weekend house of the Kaufmann family was built over a waterfall in Pennsylvania, USA. A large part of the house is supported over the river using cantilevers, which was a real challenge for the engineers of the time. This is considered to be one of Frank Lloyd Wright's masterpieces.

The house is the perfect example of the modern pavilion house. It has an open horizontal space leading on to the exterior through large openings and wide terraces that extend on concrete slabs. This makes it appear as if the house is floating above the water.

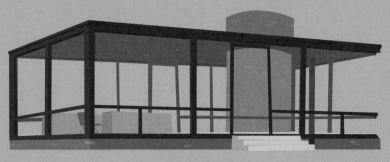

Glass House Philip Johnson 1945–49

Upper Lawn Alison and Peter Smithson 1956–62

House In Orinda Charles Moore 1962

Reinventing the modern house

Houses provide a safe space where we spend a large part of our lives. But for many centuries architects paid little attention to their design, preferring to spend their time on temples, palaces, and churches.

In today's modern world, architects have come to reflect on what houses are for and to experiment with them. With industrialization and the emergence of new technologies, people's lives have changed dramatically, and architects have had to think of ways to adapt houses to new tastes and needs. The result has been some stunning designs.

The Box Ralph Erskine 1942

E-1027 Eileen Gray 1926–29

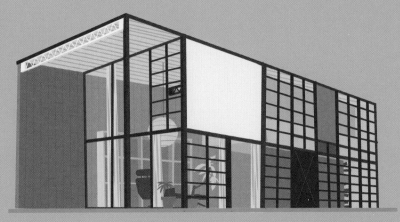

Case Study House 8 Charles and Ray Eames 1945–49

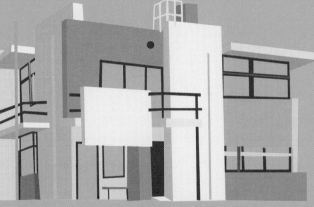

Schröder House Gerrit Rietveld 1924–25

German Pavilion
Barcelona, Spain

🕐 1929	⬤ Mies van der Rohe	▦ Marble, steel, stone, and glass	🏛 Exhibition pavilion

Ludwig Mies van der Rohe (known as Mies) and Lilly Reich designed the German Pavilion for the 1929 Barcelona International Exposition. Inspired by painter Piet Mondrian's abstract style of horizontal and vertical lines and primary colors, this building broke down the space into horizontal and vertical planes (slab roofs and walls). This created a continuous space that fused together the inside and outside of the house. The building's colors were provided by the different kinds of stone that were used.

ROOF

ENTRANCE

BLOCKS OF TRAVERTINE MARBLE GIVE A FEELING OF LUXURY AND SPACIOUSNESS

STEEL PILLARS WITH A CROSS-SHAPED SECTION

The pavilion was demolished after the exhibition but rebuilt in the 1980s in Barcelona.

When the pavilion was first opened it caused considerable surprise. No one had ever seen architecture like it.

BARCELONA CHAIR DESIGNED BY MIES FOR THE PAVILION

Ludwig Mies van der ROHE

The architecture of Mies is the best example of an "open" floor plan: airy spaces sandwiched between the floor and roof. There are no walls, just some columns or non-load-bearing walls and plain glass facades, which create a very close relationship between the inside and outside.

Mies (1886–1969) broke with the over-decorated architecture of his time. Alongside figures like Wright, Aalto, and Le Corbusier, this German architect was one of the creators of modern architecture. He was deeply influenced by the experimental avant garde art of the time. One of his maxims was "less is more." He tried to make his buildings beautiful by seeking out their essential geometric forms, with no decoration at all. In the late 1930s, he moved to the USA, where his minimalist approach was enormously influential over future architecture.

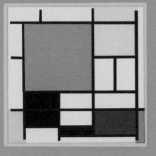

Piet Mondrian, *Composition with Red, Yellow, Blue and Black*, 1921. The abstract paintings of this Dutch artist were an important influence on Mies.

Model of the Farnsworth House

Farnsworth House, Illinois, USA, 1945–50

A classic example of Mies's North American phase, this house includes most of the characteristics of his buildings. The floor and roof are raised above the ground, held up by metal columns (in the style of classical temples) and surrounded on all four sides by glass. The house has a transparent interior, broken up only by furniture and service areas.

MR10 Cantilever chair

Aluminum chair designed by Mies.

Kimbell Art Museum Louis Kahn
Fort Worth, Texas, USA
1966–72 art gallery

Bauhaus Building Walter Gropius
Dessau, Germany 1925–26 art school

Cathedral of Brasília
Oscar Niemeyer Brasília, Brazil
1958–70 cathedral

30 St Mary Axe
(The Gherkin)
Norman Foster &
Ken Shuttleworth
London, UK
2001–03 offices

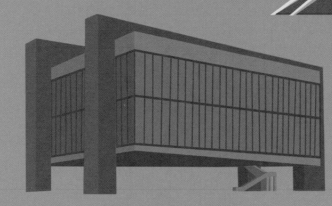

São Paulo Museum of Art Lina Bo Bardi
São Paulo, Brazil 1958–68 art gallery

Guggenheim Museum Bilbao
Frank Gehry Bilbao, Spain
1992–97 art gallery

Berlin Philharmonic Hall Hans Scharoun Berlin, Germany
1960–63 concert hall

ICONIC BUILDINGS

Throughout history, and especially during the 20th and 21st centuries, many anonymous buildings have been produced. However, there are also significant, iconic buildings that symbolize the spirit of the time. We are able to understand the architecture of the past 100 years by looking at buildings as different from each other as the Bauhaus Building by Walter Gropius or the Sydney Opera House by Jørn Utzon.

The Einstein Tower Erich Mendelsohn
Potsdam, Germany 1919–21
astrophysical observatory

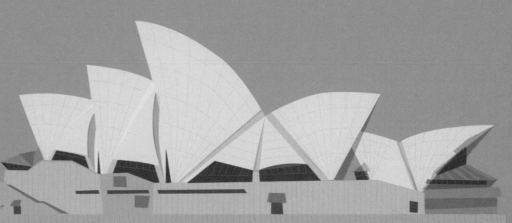

Sydney Opera House Jørn Utzon Sydney, Australia 1959–73 opera house

Solomon R. Guggenheim Museum Frank Lloyd Wright
New York, USA 1956–59 art gallery

Casa del Fascio Giuseppe Terragni
Como, Italy 1932–36 political headquarters

Structures

Buildings are able to remain standing because of the way they are designed and the materials they are made from. All structures, from houses to bridges, must be able to withstand all the weight and forces placed on them, which includes the weight of the structure itself, people, furniture, vehicles—and the impact of the wind.

To understand the importance of structure it helps to think of the human body. Our skeleton enables our body to stay upright, to walk, and to support weight. The bones in the body are like the columns and beams in a building, while the skin is like the building's facades and the roof.

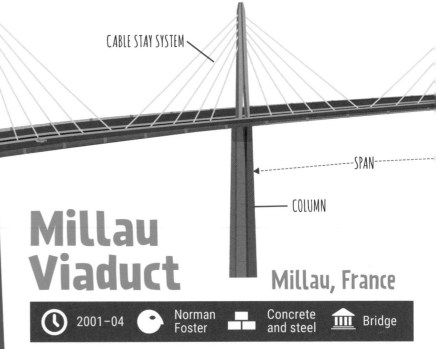

CABLE STAY SYSTEM

SPAN

COLUMN

Millau Viaduct

Millau, France

🕐 2001–04	🐦 Norman Foster	⬜ Concrete and steel	🏛 Bridge

It is very difficult to build long-span bridges because of the length of beams needed to join the piers or columns. Systems such as cable stays can increase the length of bridge possible between columns. The Millau Viaduct has six spans of 1,122ft and two spans of 670ft, covering a total length of over 1.5 miles.

MIND THE GAP

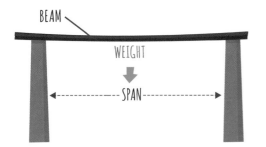

BEAM

WEIGHT

SPAN

Since prehistoric times, humans have built bridges to cross rivers and ravines. Different kinds of bridges have evolved depending on the distance they have to cross and the materials and techniques available. With industrialization and the introduction of new techniques for building with iron, bridges became large-scale engineering projects, as important as vertical structures, and the architects and engineers working on them focused on how to cross ever greater distances.

The distance between the two points that support a beam is called the "span." The longer the span, the more complicated and expensive it becomes to find a solution to cover the distance without the structure bending or breaking. In large structures, such as bridges, big spans increase the size of the structural elements needed to support them.

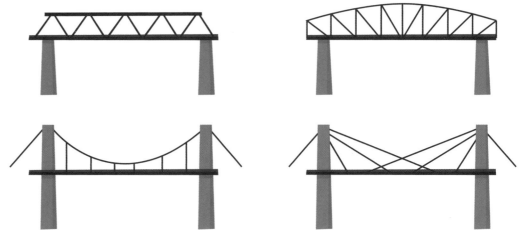

Designing structures

The strength must be calculated by considering the loads the structures have to bear (such as people, furniture, vehicles, and construction materials), the terrain they are built on (which will transmit the load into the ground) and the climate (such as wind, snow, and rain). From Ancient Greek times to today, architects and engineers have used complex formulas, theories, and methods to carry out these calculations. Trial and error has also been used—but this is costly and dangerous. Today, computer programs have made all these processes easier.

When thinking about building large-scale structures, we should also think about how and where the different structural elements are made—and how they are transported to the place where they will be used. No doubt all of us have seen trucks and trains laden with the enormous prefabricated steel or concrete beams that are needed to build large structures.

Higher and higher

Humans have always wanted to create tall structures that reach for the sky. These include Egyptian obelisks, Arab minarets, and the towers of Italy.

The first skyscrapers appeared in Chicago and New York, USA in the late 19th century. As construction techniques advanced and modern elevators were invented, more tall building were constructed, and they came to represent modern cities. These great buildings might provide housing or office space. They save space, usually in places where land is very expensive, but they also represent the political and economic power of the cities and of the companies that build them.

For this reason there is still a lot of competition about who is able to put up the tallest building. Currently, the Burj Khalifa in Dubai, United Arab Emirates, holds the record as the highest building in the world, but other buildings are being designed that could one day be more than half a mile high.

2,000ft

1,000ft

World's tallest
building
1889–1930

World's tallest
building
1998–2003

The Eiffel Tower
1,063ft Stephen Sauvestre
and Gustave Eiffel
Paris, 1889

**2 International
Finance Center**
1,362ft César Pelli Hong
Kong, 2003

432 Park Avenue
1,369ft
Rafael Viñoly
New York, 2015

Empire State Building
1,454ft Shreve,
Lamb and Harmon
New York, 1931

Petronas Towers
1,483ft César Pelli Kuala
Lumpur, 1998

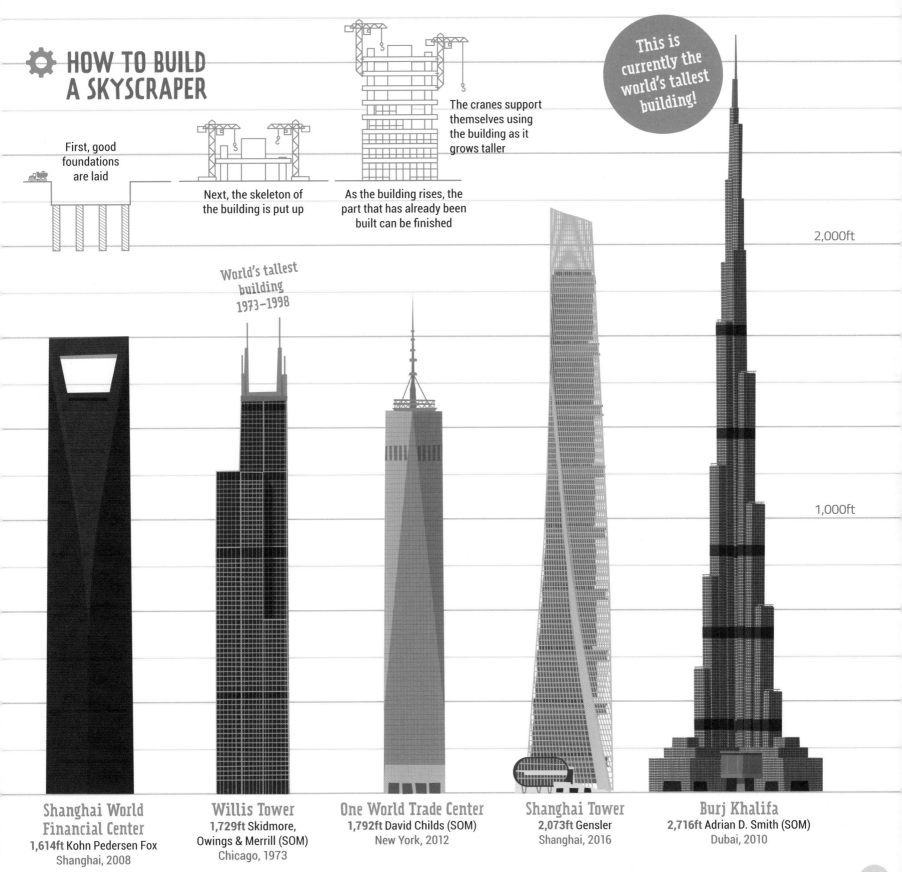

HOW TO BUILD A SKYSCRAPER

First, good foundations are laid

Next, the skeleton of the building is put up

As the building rises, the part that has already been built can be finished

The cranes support themselves using the building as it grows taller

This is currently the world's tallest building!

2,000ft

1,000ft

World's tallest building 1973–1998

Shanghai World Financial Center
1,614ft Kohn Pedersen Fox
Shanghai, 2008

Willis Tower
1,729ft Skidmore, Owings & Merrill (SOM)
Chicago, 1973

One World Trade Center
1,792ft David Childs (SOM)
New York, 2012

Shanghai Tower
2,073ft Gensler
Shanghai, 2016

Burj Khalifa
2,716ft Adrian D. Smith (SOM)
Dubai, 2010

Zaha HADID

Born in Iraq, Hadid (1950–2016) studied mathematics in Beirut and, later, architecture in London where she established her own practice. In 2004 she became the first woman to win the Pritzker Architecture Prize.

Her futuristic, passionate, overwhelming style placed her at the same level as other star architects such as Rem Koolhaas, Norman Foster, and Frank Gehry. Her plans used bold, risky, unconventional forms, and she made many innovations in furniture design, sculpture, painting, and other decorative objects.

Antwerp Port House
Zaha Hadid architects
Antwerp, Belgium 2016

The Heydar Aliyev Center
Baku, Azerbaijan

| 🕐 2007 | Zaha Hadid | 🧱 Concrete, glass, and steel | 🏛 Cultural center |

This cultural center, featuring large-scale column-free spaces, is characterized by its curved lines, which symbolize the continuity between the present, the past, and the future.

Contemporary architecture

Since 2000, contemporary architecture has become globalized. This means that although it is influenced by the culture and economy of each region, it has common characteristics worldwide.

There has always been a great difference between smaller projects and grand works. But in general, contemporary architecture is characterized by its use of new materials and technologies that allow previously unthinkable buildings to be constructed—from the curving, natural forms of the Heydar Aliyev Center to enormous skyscrapers such as Burj Khalifa. This architecture seeks to blend itself into its surroundings by using complex geometry that maintains a link with the lives and customs of its users.

FEMALE ARCHITECTS

Throughout history, women have played a significant part in designing buildings, but they did not receive the credit they deserved. Often, because of social attitudes of the time, husbands would be named as the creators of their wives' work. Thankfully over the past century many more women architects have come to the fore. These include **Lilly Reich, Jane Drew, Aino Marsio-Aalto, Ray Eames, Charlotte Perriand, Lina Bo Bardi, Denise Scott Brown, and Alison Smithson. More recently Carme Pigem, Carme Pinós, Anna Heringer, Odile Decq, and Benedetta Tagliabue have become widely known. Kazuyo Sejima became the second female winner of the Pritzker Architecture Prize in 2010 after Zaha Hadid.**

New Museum
Kazuyo Sejima and
Ryue Nishizawa
New York, USA
2002–07
art museum

Every building is different. Each design depends on a series of factors including the materials that are available, the nature of the ground, the climatic conditions, and the eventual use of the building, all set within a budget. For these reasons, it is very important for the architects and everyone else involved in the building process to use a shared technical language to avoid mistakes and misunderstandings.

In general terms the principal parts of any building are: foundations, structure, fittings, enclosure, internal divisions, and cladding.

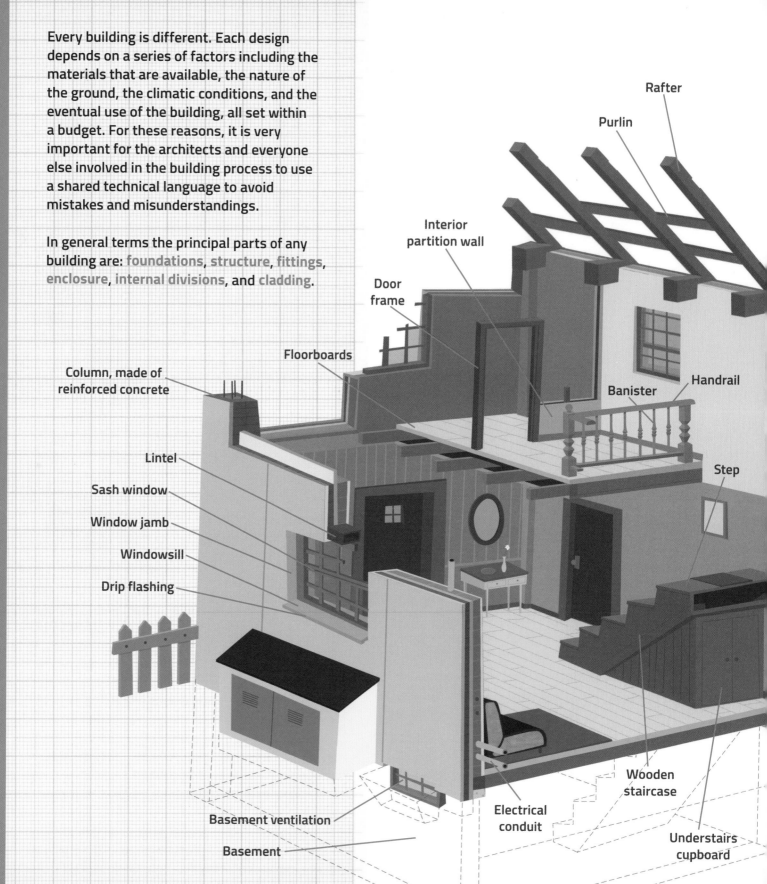

Rafter

Purlin

Interior partition wall

Door frame

Floorboards

Column, made of reinforced concrete

Lintel

Sash window

Window jamb

Windowsill

Drip flashing

Banister

Handrail

Step

Wooden staircase

Electrical conduit

Understairs cupboard

Basement ventilation

Basement

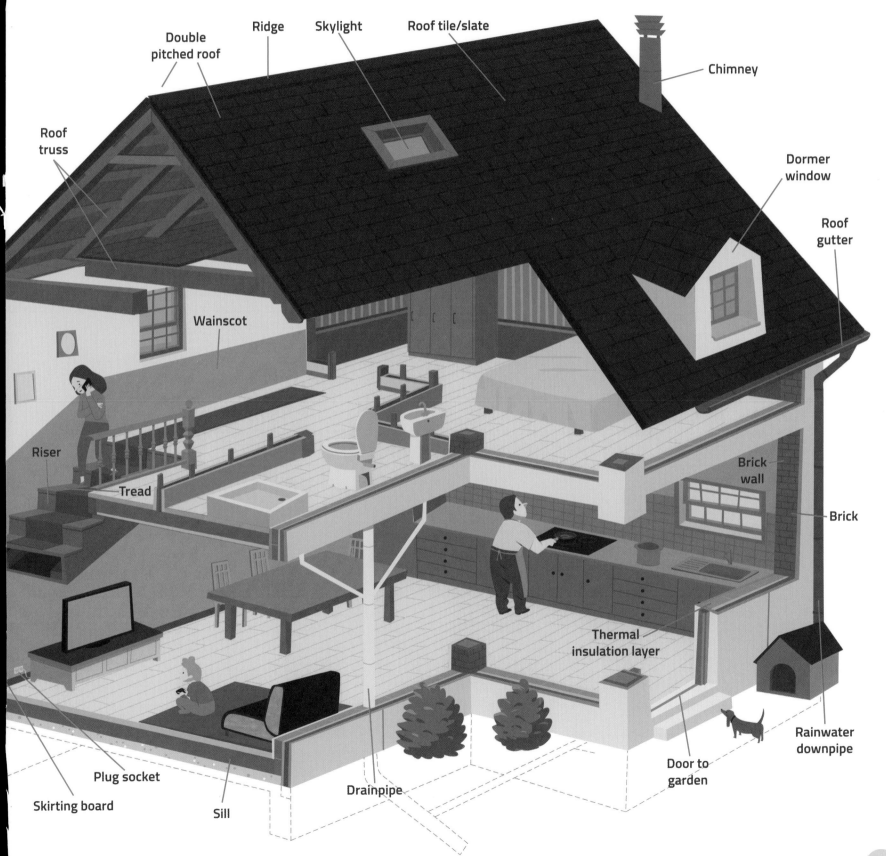

Double
pitched roof

Ridge

Skylight

Roof tile/slate

Chimney

Roof
truss

Dormer
window

Roof
gutter

Wainscot

Riser

Brick
wall

Tread

Brick

Thermal
insulation layer

Rainwater
downpipe

Plug socket

Door to
garden

Skirting board

Sill

Drainpipe

43

Being an architect

We may imagine architects working alone, guided only by their inspiration. In reality, they work in a **studio** alongside colleagues who specialize in working out structures or who are **experts** in other areas (such as safety, solar energy, downpipes, or switches). They also talk to other professionals, which encourages **collective thinking**.

During construction
Plans, scale models, and reports ensure that the project built is what the architect imagined.

Clients
Architectural projects almost always start with a client asking an architect to work for them. This can be a private individual who needs a house or a government that wants to build an entire neighborhood.

Clients are interested in the final result of the project, such as the materials used, delivery dates, and budget. Architects have to be very meticulous and keep all the promises they make to their clients.

Plans, models, and 3D projections
In order to make the plans they have in their heads real, architects must turn them into drawings and models (which they might actually make, or they may be virtual). It is important for people to be able to imagine an idea if they are going to understand how it will work.

Architect

Client

2D software

3D software

THE SKILLS ARCHITECTS NEED

Communication

Architects must know how to communicate their ideas in both words and drawings. It is important to know how to explain clearly to clients and those who work alongside you exactly what you want to achieve.

Knowledge

An architect knows about a lot of things: structures, the building process, drawing, physics, history, and town planning. All this knowledge helps a project to be successful.

Tradition

Architects should be aware that they are part of a tradition that has built up over hundreds of years. However new their work is, it should relate to what has been done before, by architects from their own culture and from elsewhere. In this way, all of us together are part of a chain of knowledge that allows us to improve our buildings, our cities, and our relationship with nature.

Would you like to be an architect?

Project archives

Architectural books

Models

Interior designer

Networking

An architectural project is a very complicated thing that needs to involve a wide range of professionals if everything is to be kept under control.

Plans

For example, one team suggests initial ideas and produces sketches, another develops the first plans and further sketches, another calculates the structures and chooses the materials, and yet another prepares the technical specifications. Finally, the technical experts take control of the actual construction process. It is the chief architect who controls all these phases and keeps the overall vision of the project in their head.

36 KINGS ROAD

Material samples

Architecture of the future

Sustainability

This is the need to find a balance between humans and our planet. The buildings we are currently making might affect the resources available for future generations. To develop sustainable architecture means thinking about our buildings in the most ecological way possible. This includes using natural materials and minimizing their impact.

What will buildings look like years from now? How will we live in them? What will cities and towns look like? No one knows for sure, but architects, town planners, and scientists agree that we will have to **respect the environment** as much as possible while creating the settlements of tomorrow.

The relation between the city and its surroundings

To avoid everyone moving to the big cities, good transport and communications need to be created between major cities and their neighboring towns.

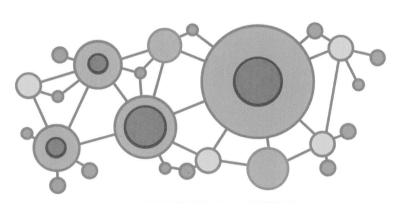

TRANSPORT HUB

FARMS

Clean energy

Renewable energy, fast transport systems (to reduce car use), and responsible industrial production will be needed if we are to create places to live that are free from pollution.

Some science fiction authors have imagined the **cities of the future** as dark places, polluted and overcrowded. Others imagine them as spacious, highly technological places where greater emphasis is placed on the welfare of the inhabitants.

How we build our towns and cities greatly influences the way we live, so it is important to recognize that all the buildings and all the people in a city are **interrelated**. It is as if they are all part of one enormous **living creature**. For this reason, architects need to work with politicians, town planners, sociologists, engineers, and citizens to create places to live that **respect** both people and the environment.

WIND TURBINE
GENERATES
ELECTRICITY

TOWN

The utopian era

In the 1960s, architects, town planners, and artists began to imagine what houses might look like in the future. Since then, many individuals and groups have put forward their ideas. These have ranged from the construction of entire neighborhoods of concrete to the proposals of organic architects to build only with natural materials.

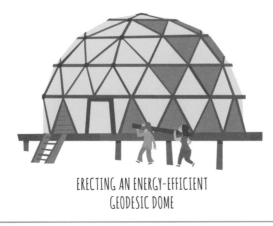

ERECTING AN ENERGY-EFFICIENT GEODESIC DOME

Information technology and new **materials** will make it possible to create structures very different from the ones we know today. New construction techniques will also emerge, such as **3D printing** of buildings.

Green growth

One idea for reducing the impact of cities is to combine the countryside and the city. This might mean that buildings become **vertical gardens** and cities are filled with parks and buildings where food is grown.

Sustainable buildings

To reduce damage to the **environment**, it is better to build in places where there have been buildings before. Some architects argue that the best way to create **sustainable** buildings and communities is to build **upwards**.

DRONE LANDING PAD

WIND TURBINE

NEW TOWN

OLD TOWN

FLOATING SOLAR PANEL

FLOATING HOUSE

FISH FARM

What do YOU think the towns and cities of the future will look like?

Life on Mars

One day, perhaps, humans will begin to live on other planets, such as Mars. In this hostile environment, the new settlers will have to trust architects, scientists, and engineers to create spaces that are safe to live in.

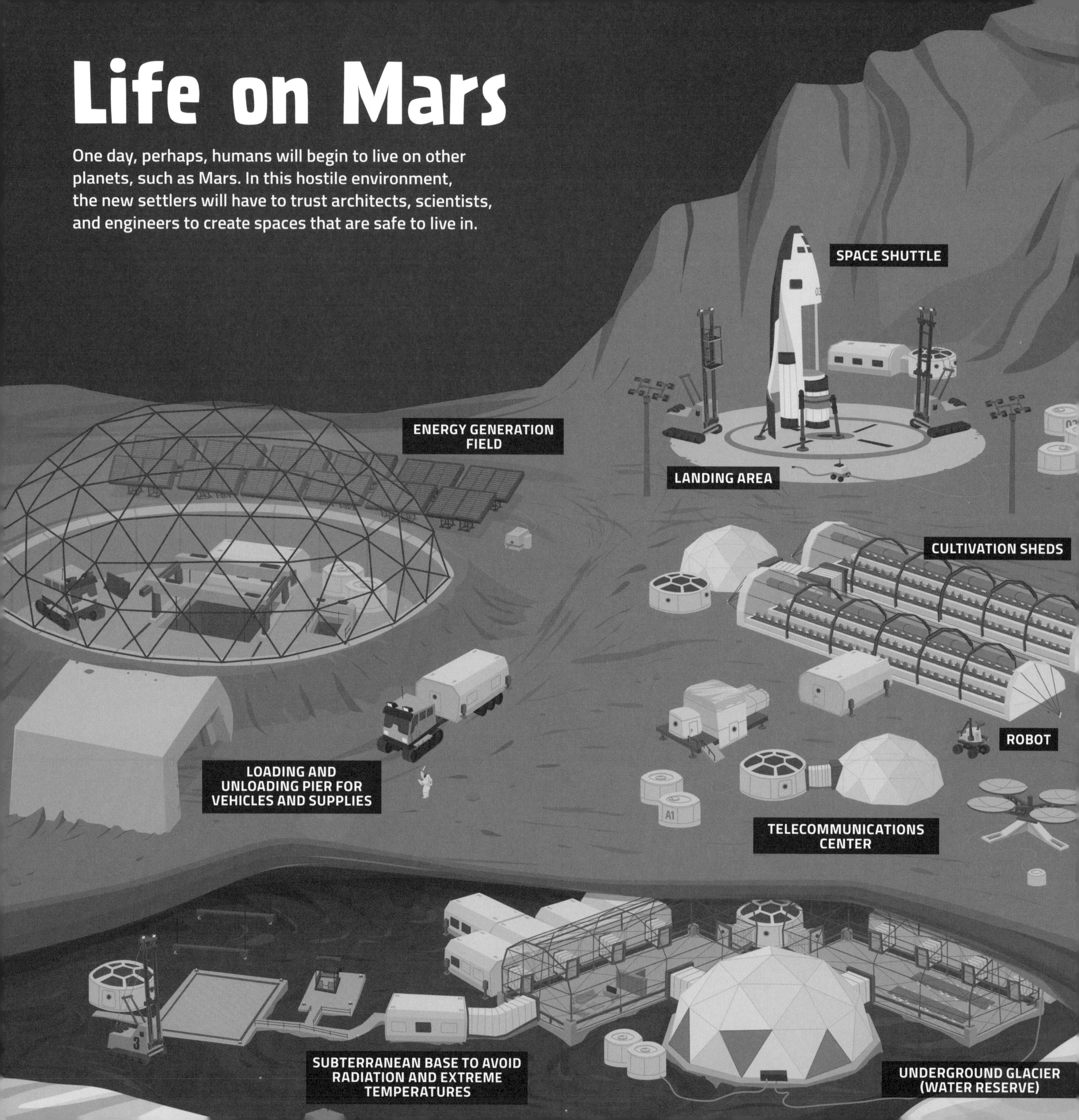

SPACE SHUTTLE

ENERGY GENERATION FIELD

LANDING AREA

CULTIVATION SHEDS

ROBOT

LOADING AND UNLOADING PIER FOR VEHICLES AND SUPPLIES

TELECOMMUNICATIONS CENTER

SUBTERRANEAN BASE TO AVOID RADIATION AND EXTREME TEMPERATURES

UNDERGROUND GLACIER (WATER RESERVE)

THE SOLOMON R GUGGENHEIM MUSEUM